ABOUT GEORGE

George Ostrom is the author of
Glacier's Secrets I & II and *Wondrous Wildlife.*

He is a longtime columnist for the
Hungry Horse News,
a newsman/radio personality, photographer,
University of Montana Distinguished Alumni,
and inductee/member of the
Montana Broadcasters Hall of Fame.

****

Contact: ggeorgeostrom@gmail.com

ISBN: 978-1-59152-228-7

For more information or to order extra copies of this book call Farcountry Press toll free at (800) 821-3874.

sweetgrassbooks
a division of Farcountry Press

Produced by Sweetgrass Books
PO Box 5630, Helena, MT 59604; (800) 821-3874;
www.sweetgrassbooks.com

Produced and printed in the United States of America.

22 21 20 19 18 1 2 3 4 5

MOUNTAIN GOAT

'Til winter coats shed, rather late in July,
Mother goats seek cool places to lie.

The kid wants a nap, but NOT on cold snow.
So up on mom seems the best place to go.

MOOSE

Kershomp kershomp she came at night
Out of a forest where skeeters bite.

Entered the village some shrubs to eat,
Something yummy along each street.

On 2nd Street one lady arose,
To see at her window a large fuzzy nose.

"Police! Police! Come rescue me!"
"Well, tell us what that critter might be?"

"Heaven knows, well golly dear me!
It's the ugliest horse I ever did see."

Kershomp kershomp
she left at first light.

Back in the woods,
a beautiful sight.

BUFFALO

Bonkity Bonkity toro toes, huge humpy bumpy old buffaloes.

They bellow and roar and snort and snore.
Eat lots of grass and then look for some more.

Wallow in the dust to remove flies and crust.
Then guzzle water 'til they darn near bust.

Bonkity Bonkity toro toes, huge humpy bumpy old buffaloes.

MULE DEER

Yummy yum yahooey, see the colors all so chewy.
Muleys chomp on pretty flowers, then munch 'em by the hours.

Doesn't matter red or blue, yellow's also good to chew.
They love the alpine lilies and think daisies are the dillies.

If you see some hungry deers, wearing big humongous ears,
Tell 'em, **"Yummy yum yahooey,** see the colors all so chewy."

BIGHORN SHEEP

In **Whomp Whomp** autumn weather, rams bang their horns together.
They crash like speeding trains, which dizzies up their brains.

Colliding racks make deafening "CRACKS," among the mountains high.
Then the winners get the ladies and the losers sulk nearby.

In **Whomp Whomp** autumn weather, rams bang their horns together.

BLACK BEAR

Golly golly glunk. There's a Beasty on that trunk.
It's a curious little Bear and it shimmied way up there.

When it needs some yummy eats, the Best are natural treats.
'Cause if people offer goodies to her cub there in the woodies,

Mother Bear comes growling out and will cuff them 'round about.
Golly golly glunk. There's a Beasty on that trunk.

MOUNTAIN LION

Blooskitty Blooskitty, Blooskitty Blam, there's a lion on the lam.

'Tis a panther on a spree, climbing up in a big old tree.

Trouble started when Slim Pickin's

Led him to dine on neighbor's chickens.

To avoid bad trouble, 'twas best to flee,

Far far away, then rest in a tree.

Blooskitty Blooskitty, Blooskitty Blam, there's a lion on the lam.

BLUEBIRDS

Utterly flutterly, Bright thrushes sing By.
Oh golly! They're BlueBirds, the flowers that fly.

Mother gets Babies from eggs CoBalt Blue,
While father Brings food as good Daddys Do.

From early Dawn hours 'neath the sun's warming rays,
The thrush's Cheerful songs Proclaim happiness Days.

When nights grow long, summer's tunes are all gone,
"Over the RainBow"...or somePlace Beyond.

OWLS

Scowly Prowly Owly hunts rodent things, during night on silent wings.
Gets his sleep while dark's away. One of 'em napped on a post all day.

We studied him for almost an hour, wondering why he looked so sour.
It's likely been a long, long while since anyone saw an owly smile.

Scowly Prowly Owly hunts rodent things, during night on silent wings.

WHITETAIL DEER

Scads of spots and speckles—Why does that fawn have freckles?

Perhaps she has the measles or the chicken pox with spleasles.

NO! That's not the reason. It's the baby hiding season.

When she naps down in the bushes and doesn't move a hair,

Nothing big can find her, not a coyote, lion, or bear.

Scads of spots and speckles—that's why the fawn has freckles.

PRONGHORN ANTELOPE

Varoom Varoom oh Darnie Boom, give that antelope running room.
He wins at animal racing meets, 'cause every Beast he really Beats.

He might outrun the fastest cheetah, even if the cheetah cheated.

Danger is signaled with white rump flashes,
sending his herd on runaway dashes.

Varoom Varoom oh Darnie Boom, give that antelope running room.

ELK

Hoogle yoogle snoogle, why does the bull elk bugle?

He's sending out a call for a wife to love this fall.
Doesn't matter big or small, 'cause he'll love 'em one and all.

His appetite's on the blink with hardly time for sleep and drink.
Other bulls a sneakin' 'round, better heed his warning sound.

Hoogle yoogle snoogle, that's why the bull elk bugle.

WOLF

Flibbering thru the fleeby tulf, trots a hungry lobo wolf.
Something we must understand, he doesn't live near a burger stand.

Cares not he for cake and tea. "Fries and shakes are not for me.
Never scared Red Riding Hood, or ate her grandma in that snood."

After catching a few fat mice, howling at the moon is nice.
Flibbering thru the fleeby tulf, trots a wily lobo wolf.

MOUNTAIN GOATS

Screezee scrocks, screezee scrocks,
Mountain goats live on the high, high rocks.

The mommas' winter coats are way too hot,
So warm spring sun makes them shed a lot.

Kids climb the cliffs, playing king of the hill.
Jumping off steep places, just for drill.

Screezee scrocks, screezee scrocks,
Mountain goats live on the high, high rocks.

COYOTE

A slinky super prowler and a dandy nighttime howler,
Only one thing this could be; bet your boots a coyotee.

Raises furry puppies in home dug holes
Feeds 'em on gophers and fuzzy gray voles.

They travel in packs, without toothpaste or sacks
And catch crunchy crickets for in-between snacks.

A slinky super prowler and a dandy nighttime howler.

THE CUB GRIZ

Wahwah, wahwah, wahwah Blues,
The teenage grizzly needs some shoes.

Look at the soles, he shows us all.
"I'd find something better, but we have no mall.

I've got good claws and teeth and all.
I'll grow new soles, by early this fall."

Wahwah, wahwah,
wahwah Blues,
The teenage grizzly
needs some shoes.

BEAVER

We're webfoot willow weavers, Bark-Biting Busy Beavers.
Block up babbling cricks, with gunk and gooey sticks,

So we can make deep dams, for raising sons and daughters,
And forming pretty ponds, for trout and moose and otters.

Gnaw down big green trees to eat the twigs and leaves.
Working night and day, with scanty time for play.

We're webfoot willow weavers, Bark-Biting Busy Beavers.

(Photo courtesy of Chris Peterson, Hungry Horse News)

BADGER

Cagey Clawing Cadger, the Beady-eyed Bold Badger.
Got stubby little tails but long and tough toenails.

Can dig a burrow and close 'r, faster than a diesel dozer.
This young one is curious...should it act quite nice or furious?

Badgers have few friends on the prairies or the glens,
So they challenge any stranger, whether rattler, rat or ranger.

Cagey Clawing Cadger, the Beady-eyed Bold Badger.

WATER OTTERS

Here's a mother otter
And her fully grownup daughter.

They eat what they have sought here,
Catching trout in icy water.

They slide down slippery banks
And laugh at silly pranks.

Life is fun for playful otters.
They'd love our teeter totters.

BABY MOOSE

'Tis not a time for fun, for this cow moose's son.
Learning to cross wild streams can give a calf bad dreams.

"Maybe it's too deep, or the bank o'er there's too steep."
But! Mother is the boss and she picked this place to cross.

Regardless of his fright, he must keep his mom in sight.
That's what you learn in schools, where Mother Nature rules.

GRIZZLY BEAR

Fleegle fleegle flottom,
There's a grizzly Bear's Bottom.

He can't get tasty honey
For free or even money.

So he sneaks it from wild Bees,
'Neath the logs and hollow trees,

While they sting him on the elbows,
On the hindy and the knees.

Fleegle fleegle flottom,
Oh! That Poor Bear's Bottom.

THIS IS THE END

ZANY, BRAINY ANIMALS

HOW ANIMALS DEFEND THEMSELVES

DR. ASHLEY WARD AND ANDY ROWLAND

PowerKiDS press

Published in 2026
by The Rosen Publishing Group, Inc.
2544 Clinton Street, Buffalo, NY 14224

First published in Great Britain in 2024 by Wayland

Editor: Elise Short
Designer: Rachel Lawston

Cataloging-in-Publication Data

Names: Ward, Ashley, author. | Rowland, Andy, 1962-, illustrator.
Title: How animals defend themselves / by Dr. Ashley Ward, illustrated by Andy Rowland.
Description: Buffalo, NY : PowerKids Press, 2026. | Series: Zany, brainy animals | Includes glossary and index.
Identifiers: ISBN 9781499454154 (pbk.) | ISBN 9781499454161 (library bound) | ISBN 9781499454178 (ebook)
Subjects: LCSH: Animal defenses--Juvenile literature. | Animals--Adaptation--Juvenile literature. | Animal behavior--Juvenile literature. | Camouflage (Biology)--Juvenile literature.

Classification: LCC QL759.W373 2026 | DDC 591.47--dc23

Manufactured in the United States of America
CPSIA Compliance Information: Batch #CSPK26. For further information contact Rosen Publishing at 1-800-237-9932.

Picture credits:
Alamy: Ethan Daniels13t,Laura Romin & Larry Dalton 15c. Shutterstock: Aastels 10t, Allexxandar13b b/g, Evgeny Ayupov 9tr, Brent Barnes 20tr, Bear Fotos 20cl, Audrey Snider-Bell 26t,Randy Bjorklund 8br, Mark Bridger 10b, Yulia Burkarova 8t, Chainfoto24 4c,18c, Craig Dingle 22t, Ashton Ea 6, Foreverhappyfr cover b,Tyler Fox 8bl, GypsyPictureShow 23br, Happy monkey 15b, Eric Isselee 19b, Rosa Jay 5b, IrinaK 24, Irin-k 11tl, Randi Kayu 19tr, Prahab Louilarpprasert 9bl, Fabio Maffei 16t, Benny Marty 26bl, Liz Miller 28t, Jay Ondreika 25t, Pakhnyushchy 17c,Vadim Petrakov 21t, 21b, Pinosub 7b,PRILL 28b, SoFlo Shots 5t, 23tr, Nickolay Stanev 29t,David Pineda Svenske 23tl, Johan Swanepoel 14bl,Torook 27b, Wildestanimal 29b. Wikimedia Commons: Dan Schofield 12b, CCA 4.0 International.

CONTENTS

HOW DO ANIMALS DEFEND THEMSELVES?

For lots of animals, life can sometimes be dangerous. So, to keep themselves safe, animals have to defend themselves. There are many different ways of doing this of course, from being **SUPERFAST** to **SUPERSTRONG** and from being **SUPERSMART** to **SUPER SNEAKY!**

In this book, we'll look at the fascinating ways in which animals defend themselves, fooling their enemies to make sure that they win the game of life.

TALES FROM THE LAB

Understanding animal behavior is not an easy task. First, scientists watch animals living their life. That's how they get their ideas. Then they test these ideas by running experiments. If they're lucky, they'll find out something that no one has ever known about animals, which is the most exciting thing possible! In this book, you'll find many amazing discoveries about how animals defend themselves.

CAMOUFLAGE

One of the best ways to avoid being discovered by a hungry predator is to blend into the background, a sneaky strategy known as camouflage.

Some animals, like the leafy sea dragon, take this to such extreme lengths that you might not see it even when you're looking straight at it. Part of the reason is that the sea dragon is exactly the same color as the seaweed that it lives in. It can even change color to make sure it blends in.

In addition to this, the sea dragon has evolved a **VERY STRANGE** shape. Sprouting from its body are all sorts of special growths that make it look less like a fish and more like seaweed.

Added to that, the sea dragon sways backward and forward in the water currents. Again, just like seaweed.

All in all, the sea dragon is a **MASTER OF DISGUISE**, hiding in plain sight, safe in the knowledge that predators, such as sharks, can't eat it if they can't find it.

One of the weirdest kinds of camouflage is used by the lemon damsel. It's weird because these coral reef fish are bright yellow. But although they stand out to us, the kinds of fish that eat lemon damsels have very different vision than humans and, to their eyes, a lemon damsel seems to be a gray color that blends into the background.

MIMICRY AND MASQUERADE

There's more than one way to change your appearance. While camouflage works for some creatures, plenty of others pretend to be something they're not, by mimicking (copying) or masquerading (disguising themselves) as another animal.

The caterpillar of the swallowtail butterfly looks exactly like bird poop. This strategy works really well, because ...

WHO WANTS TO EAT POOP?

Some of the best masqueraders are the many different species of fly who pretend to be their own worst enemy: spiders. Snowberry flies, for instance, have patterns on their wings that look exactly like spider legs.

Whenever the fly is approached by a spider, all it has to do is to stick its wings out at either side and, the fly looks like a pretty big spider, complete with **EXTREMELY HAIRY LEGS**.

Completely fooled and suddenly in fear for its own life, the real spider turns and runs away, leaving the fly to enjoy its afternoon.

TALES FROM THE LAB

For a long time, the patterns on some insects' wings were thought to simply be a way for creatures of the same species to recognize each other. That is, until clever zoologists (animal scientists) realized that they looked like something else: their predator! In experiments carried out on a type of fly, scientists wiped off the patterns on the flies' wings and found that predators didn't flee as often. Instead, they pounced!

DON'T EAT ME, I'M POISONOUS

If you're an animal small enough to be eaten, such as a little frog, one thing that might save you is if you taste awful or, better still, if you're poisonous.

The thing is, the frog doesn't want to actually be eaten for the predator to find out that it's the very opposite of delicious. The frog wants to make sure it gets the message across **LOUD AND CLEAR** before any chewing takes place.

As a result, animals like the poison arrow frog go into advertising. They sport bright colors that make them stand out and tell any potential predator that it would be a **TERRIBLE IDEA** to eat them. And since they want to be sure that there's no mistake, different poisonous animals often feature the same colors.

A combination of yellow and black is a very popular kind of warning color combo in the animal kingdom–think wasps, bees, snakes, and the list goes on. These animals all benefit from a kind of universal signal that shouts out, **"DON'T EAT ME OR YOU'LL REGRET IT!"**

Strange though it might seem, some of the poisons that animals use are really valuable to us. Scientists have carefully developed medicines from these dangerous substances and some are now used to treat things like heart problems and diabetes, and even as a remedy for pain!

HIDING

One of the simplest options available to animals that feel threatened is to hide. Lots of animals build shelters or dig burrows to keep themselves safe from harm. Thousands of years ago, our ancient ancestors lived in caves, partly out of fear of scary animals like **SABER-TOOTHED TIGERS!**

But what if you're not very good at digging or making your own refuge? That's when animals have to get creative. One of the **WEIRDEST** examples of this is the pearlfish, which, when threatened, does something truly **BIZARRE**: it hides inside a sea cucumber's bottom.

Sea cucumbers are often quite large, slow-moving animals that protect themselves using nasty-tasting or poisonous chemicals. Very few animals eat them, which is exactly why the pearlfish chooses them as its hiding place.

It's not known whether pearlfish think it's **ICKY** inside a sea cucumber's bum, but one thing's for sure: it's better than getting eaten!

Although animals go into hiding when they're in danger, some animals carry their shelter around with them. Hermit crabs have quite soft bodies, so they use old snail shells to hide in, curling the back half of their body inside the spiraling shell.

I SEE YOU!

Predators like to sneak up on their prey, stealthily creeping closer and closer, until they're almost on top of their victim before launching an attack. The **SECRET** to being a successful hunter is to make sure not to be spotted.

Most prey animals keep a wary eye out for exactly this kind of sly behavior. If they detect approaching danger, they run off at top speed in the opposite direction.

Running isn't always the best strategy though. It uses up precious energy and it means that you end up in a place you might not actually want to be. So, rather than run when they spot an advancing predator, animals like Thomson's gazelles simply let that predator know that they've seen it.

In a behavior known as "stotting," a gazelle jumps into the air repeatedly, bouncing up and down like **CRAZY** until its predator gets the message. The crucial element of surprise has been lost and it won't be catching this gazelle today.

It's vitally important for prey animals to be able to spot when a predator is sneaking up on them. You might have noticed that animals such as rabbits or sheep have eyes on the sides of their head. This means they have the widest visual field and can see almost all the way around them.

SURPRISE!

Some animals turn the tables on their attackers, giving them a nasty surprise that makes the predator think **TWICE**.

Imagine you're a snake, creeping up on what looks like a delicious and defenseless frog. **"This is too easy!"** you think to yourself as you slither closer and get ready to strike.

Suddenly, the frog, a Cuyaba dwarf frog, does a **WEIRD BIT OF YOGA** that involves sticking its bum in the air. Best of all, the frog has what looks like a pair of great big eyes on its behind, so the snake now finds itself looking at what appears to be the face of a much larger animal.

All of this is too much for the snake, which changes its mind about attacking and scoots away, defeated by a **TOTALLY TERRIFYING FROG** with a face on its bum.

It's one thing to surprise a predator in broad daylight, but how can you do this if you live in the dark? The burrowing owl, which nests underground, has a neat solution. If a dangerous animal comes to the burrow, the owls make **hissing** and **rattling** noises that convince the intruder there's a deadly rattlesnake hiding within!

TOO BIG TO EAT

With a bit of sneaky trickery, a bite-sized animal can transform itself in an instant into something that's too hefty to handle.

Puffer fish are famous for this. It's where their name comes from. One moment this little fish might be swimming along, minding its own business, when suddenly a predator appears with a nasty glint in its eye.

In the blink of an eye, the once small puffer fish drinks down a huge amount of water and expands up to three times its original size. Some puffer fish even have spikes!

The **MEGA-INFLATED** puffer is far too big for the predator to get its mouth around, so puffer fish is off the menu. It's a great defense, but don't try it yourself. It only works for puffer fish!

Have you ever seen a cat get really scared? it arches its back, its fur stands up, and its tail goes bushy. Just like the puffer fish, this makes the cat seem bigger and more daunting to its enemies!

LET'S GET OUT OF HERE!

When danger threatens, the best option can be to just get out of the way. Lots of prey animals can run–or swim, or fly–out of trouble incredibly quickly. Other animals take this a step further and simply disappear.

This is no magic trick, even if it does completely fool hungry predators. Flying fish can leap out of the water and glide away through the air, while a kind of deer, the water chevrotain, does the opposite and hides underwater. The effect is the same. The animals disappear from the view of whatever's chasing them.

The pebble toad has one more trick. This teeny amphibian lives in hilly areas, and when a large, scary spider approaches, **IT TURNS ITSELF INTO A BOUNCY BALL!**

First, the toad tucks its head, arms, and legs against its body. Then, because the toads live on steep slopes, they simply roll downhill out of danger, gathering speed as they go and leaving the spider far behind.

ARMORED ANIMALS

People have built castles to keep their enemies out for centuries, but animals came up with the idea long before we did.

Whenever you go to the seaside, you'll see plenty of animals with shells, from mussels and urchins to oysters and crabs. And if you go to Australia, you might see wombats, which have **BONY PLATES ON THEIR BUMS.** If threatened, they can stick their heads into their burrows and rely on their reinforced rear to protect them from harm.

But the most impressive of all armored creatures are tortoises. Their shell is like a fortress that covers their whole body, except for holes allowing their legs and head to poke out. And if a predator makes an unwelcome appearance, the tortoise can pull everything inside its shell, leaving its enemies with nothing but a **TOOTH-SHATTERINGLY TOUGH** suit of armor to contemplate.

Tortoises have some rivals for the title of toughest animal. The ironclad beetle's armor is so robust that it can survive a car driving over it. And the pangolin, a scaly mammal found in Asia and Africa, is so well protected by its scales that it is being used as the inspiration for body armor for people!

PLAYING DEAD

One weird way to avoid being eaten is to be **SO DISGUSTING** that no self-respecting predator would want to deal with you.

This is what the Virginia opossum does. If it finds itself in a tight spot, it rolls onto its side and **PRETENDS TO BE DEAD.** The opossum is a great actor and is really quite convincing. It even slows its breathing down. Most predators like their food to be fresh, so playing dead puts them off.

But just to be double sure, the opossum takes extra measures to deter predators. It drools and its tongue lolls out. Worse still, **A HORRIBLE, STINKY, GREEN FLUID** leaks from its bottom. In other words, it makes itself so repulsive that even the hungriest of predators think twice before digging into such a nasty meal.

Once its enemy has retreated, the opossum springs to its feet, cleans itself off, and gets back to its business.

Scientists have discovered that the reason why animals like the opossum play dead is because lots of predatory animals are attracted to movement. It takes nerves of steel to stay still when something scary is approaching, but if you can't hide or outrun your enemy, freezing might mean it'll pass right by.

FIGHTING BACK

Tarantulas–the hefty, hairy spiders found in warmer parts of the world–are pretty **FEARSOME** to look at. They're about the size of your hand and they have sharp, curved fangs that could BITE right through an unwary finger.

You might not think that there'd be many animals who would mess with them. But surprisingly, quite a few creatures, including lizards, birds, and foxes, see tarantulas as a **TASTY MEAL.**

Any hopeful spider-snacker will need to have its wits about it because the tarantula has a special attack. When its enemies get too close, the tarantula **FIRES HAIRS**, called urticating hairs, out of its bum–straight into their face.

Being hit with bum hair is no joke. Each hair is like a tiny arrow, coated with venom that'll make any would-be attacker think twice about a tarantula meal in future.

TALES FROM THE LAB

In the 1970s, tarantulas were becoming popular as pets. Thought to be safe to humans, they seemed to be causing rashes. So to be sure, in 1972, a spider scientist firmly rubbed the hairy back of a tarantula against his arm and, sure enough, an itchy rash came up. All in the name of science!

MOBBING

Imagine for a moment that you're a baby buffalo, scampering around in the sunshine on the plains of Africa. You trot past a thicket of trees when suddenly a lion bursts from cover and comes charging towards you with a hungry look in its eye. You're in **TROUBLE!**

Luckily, buffaloes live in big groups. Your mom–and most likely, the whole extended buffalo family–will be keeping watch. The lion might be thinking of you as an easy meal, right up until the moment when a huge, very angry mama appears at your side.

You're joined moments later by dozens of your friends and suddenly this has turned into a **VERY BAD DAY** for the lion. Faced with an army of huge, powerful, and decidedly furious buffaloes—all of which are armed with **WICKED HORNS**—the lion has to run for its life.

You've had a lucky escape, but it just goes to show that there's strength in numbers. When one buffalo is threatened with danger, its friends come to the rescue.

TALES FROM THE LAB

You might not think that an animal as large as a sperm whale would need to worry about predators, but killer whales can sometimes threaten young calves. Marine biologists have seen adult sperm whales gather in a circle to protect their little ones, and thrash with their tails to deter the killer whales.

GLOSSARY

Behavior the way a person or animal acts

Blend in to look or seem the same as the surroundings and not be easily noticeable

Burrow a hole in the ground dug by an animal to live in

Camouflage the way that the color or shape of an animal or plant appears to mix with its surroundings in order to prevent it from being seen and attacked

Marine biologist a scientist who studies animal, plant, and microscopic life in oceans

Masquerade the act of wearing a disguise and pretending to be something else

Mimicry the act of copying the sounds or behavior of a particular animal

Mobbing a behavior where a group of prey approach, scare, and sometimes attack a predator

Poisonous having to do with an animal making a harmful or deadly substance in its body in order to defend itself

Predator an animal that hunts other animals for food

Prey an animal that is hunted or caught for food, usually by another animal

Strategy a way of doing something or dealing with something

FURTHER INFORMATION

Books

Animals in Disguise by Michael Bright (Wayland, 2023)

How Not to Get Eaten: More than 75 Incredible Animal Defenses
by Josette Reeves (DK, 2022)

Science-ology!: Zoology
by Anna Claybourne (PowerKids Press, 2025)

Websites

Explore zoology, the study of animals though articles and games:
www.amnh.org/explore/ology/zoology

Check out lots of animal information and pictures:
https://kids.nationalgeographic.com/animals

INDEX

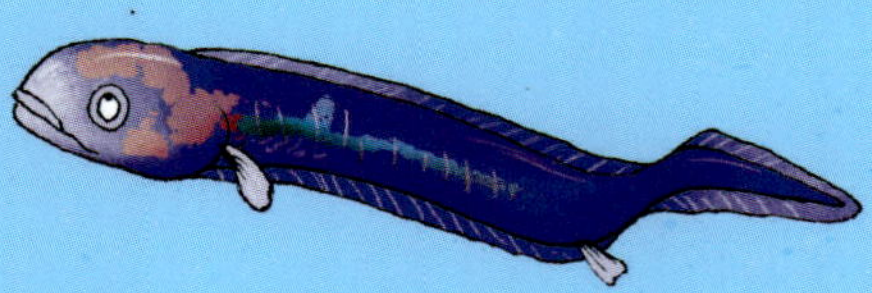